AFTER A
MILLION
QUOTES

REFLECTIONS ON APPLYING WISE
QUOTES TO LIVING WELL

A Request

I would greatly appreciate you taking a moment to review this book on Amazon.

ABOUT THIS BOOK

After years of interest in and study of practical philosophy—the kind of philosophy that can be most directly applied to living life well—I set out to write a book about what I had learned. It did not take me long to realize that much of what I wanted to say has already been said by others, often more concisely and memorably than I would have said it. The more I wrote, the clearer this became, and the more interest I developed in reading quality quotes.

As I continued to write and to read quotes, this book evolved to include many quotes. The selected quotes get at some of the most important takeaways I've found in the countless quotes I have read. I have organized this book into numerous distinct sections that all begin with a quote. Each quote is followed by my own commentary. Sometimes my commentary is to clarify the quotes, and sometimes it is to add my own ideas that complement them or take them a step further.

It is notable that I chose not to group the sections into broader categories and that I was not overly concerned with the order of the sections, although there is some logic to the order. Life rarely comes at us in an orderly fashion, and forcing too much order into a book focused on how to live well would be counterproductive. My hope is that not having excessive order will help highlight apparent contradictions between some of the quotes, and lead you to resolve these contradictions in ways that bring you insights. The physicist Neils Bohr once said, "The opposite of a correct statement is a false statement. But the opposite of a profound truth may well be another profound truth." As we read quotes, we must keep this in mind and we must also remember that many contradictions are not glaring, but subtle in nature. If we are attentive, quotes have the potential to show us how we might take other quotes too far. As I depict on the cover, quotes can balance each other out.

I hope that you take a lot from these quotes and from my commentary. I hope that this book makes you think and leads you to epiphanies. Most ambitiously, I hope that this book leads you to a greater interest in wisdom and practical philosophy that helps put you on a lifelong path to living better and better.

The only fence against the world is a thorough knowledge of it.
— John Locke

There are so many ways we can be tested in life. We can get so much right and yet have disastrous consequences from getting a few things wrong. To give ourselves the best opportunity to live well, we don't need to acquire a thorough knowledge of everything, but it is necessary for us to learn many, many important things. There is no secret to life, and we should not look for one.

The root of suffering is attachment.
— Often attributed to Buddha

We should be careful about anchoring to any outcome that we cannot control—even when we will likely get what we want. Preferring one outcome over another is fine, but we should work to not be crushed by an outcome that is not our preference. We should also apply this line of thinking to what we already have in our lives. This could be our possessions, our jobs, our social status, friends and loved ones—nearly anything. If we become too attached to something, we set ourselves up to be crushed should we ever lose it, and even if we never lose it, the fear of losing it can be devastating. We should be grateful for the good things we have in our lives but not be overly attached to them.

This is the highest wisdom that I own; freedom and life are earned by those alone who conquer them each day anew.
— Johann Wolfgang von Goethe

Forming good habits and discovering how to live well can make life easier but not effortless. There are many things that we can resolve to do, practice many times, and still be unable to do effortlessly. Such things will never become fully automatic, and we may need to renew our commitments to them frequently all our lives. Even good habits that become nearly effortless for a time can later be disrupted by changing circumstances. We must be prepared for this and ready to reinitiate important habits that have been broken. The following are some of our lifelong duties that we must continuously remind ourselves of and practice. We must remember to:

- Be grateful for the good we have in our lives and have had in the past.
- Appreciate the benefits of struggles we are currently overcoming.
- Not be bothered much by little worries or troubles.
- Maintain a good attitude and good mood most of the time.
- Give others a reasonable benefit of the doubt.
- Remind ourselves how little we really know, frequently.
- Enjoy life today, not letting the past or fears for the future prevent us from having joy now.
- Keep learning and keep improving, for life.

Wise venturing is the most commendable part of human prudence.
— George Savile

Before making an important decision, we should ensure that we have put a reasonable effort into getting enough information to choose wisely. But no matter how much information we have, it is not possible to be completely sure about most things. We have to take reasonable risks to live well. We must not demand absolute certainty before making decisions. Rather, we should seek sufficient certainty for what the situation demands.

Just as there are stupid bets that win, there are smart ones that lose. Bad decisions are not equivalent to decisions that turn out poorly. We can make good decisions and fail, and we can make bad decisions and succeed. We must beware of excessively judging our decisions by outcome alone. We must differentiate between decisions that were smart but end in bad results and decisions that were poor and end in bad results. As the Roman philosopher and politician Marcus Cicero put it, "We must not say that every mistake is a foolish one." Better yet, perhaps it is better to not think of smart bets that turn out poorly as "mistakes" at all.

You will never find time for anything. If you want time, you must make it.
— Charles Buxton

We have a massive cognitive bias that makes most of us believe it will be much easier in the future to take the actions needed to improve ourselves. We readily believe we will have much more free time and energy to make needed changes. We must become very aware of and very intolerant of such beliefs. We cannot foolishly assume that it will be much easier to take the actions we most need to in the future. It probably won't be. If we want to be assured of a successful, happier future, we have to develop ourselves now and work toward important goals now, rather than depending on our doing so at some point down the road.

If you wish to live, you must first attend your own funeral.
— Katherine Mansfield

Living well requires that we accept our eventual death, and it requires us to accept that it could come much sooner than we would like. We may never be completely comfortable with this, but we must not avoid thinking about it. To the contrary, we would do well to remind ourselves frequently that we are mortal and that our time is quite limited. This is not to encourage recklessness. It is to help us to prioritize well and not be bothered excessively by little things. We should care much less about living a long life and much more about living life well. To a large degree, how long we live is out of our control. How well we live is much more controllable.

Perseverance is a great element of success. If you only knock long enough and loud enough at the gate, you are sure to wake up somebody.
— Henry Wadsworth Longfellow

Innate ability, intelligence, and talent are much less responsible for success than we often think. Sustained effort and persistence are much more important than is commonly recognized. With enough determination, enough time, and enough effort, we can accomplish much. The philosopher William James once noted that "Men habitually use only a small part of the powers they possess and which they might use under appropriate circumstances." With enough persistence, most of us have amazing capability. Recognizing this, even a little bit, makes us more likely to tap into some of this power.

As we work toward goals, we should be aware that initial failure in an endeavor often does not say much about our ability to accomplish it in the long run. However, as we are persistent in our efforts to accomplish a goal, we must remember to be willing to try many different methods to achieve it, as any single method may be ineffective.

"What I believe" is a process rather than a finality.
— Emma Goldman

In a sense, everything we believe or disbelieve has a probability, ranging from something we think is very unlikely to something we are almost positive about. How strongly we believe or disbelieve something should be closely related to the evidence for or against the thing. Accordingly, we should only let ourselves believe that something is very likely true if we have considerable evidence that it is true. And we should be far from positive about something we have only moderate evidence for.

Our beliefs, and the strength of our beliefs should be continuously updated as we get new evidence. We should be careful about what we allow ourselves to feel absolutely certain is or is not true, as such beliefs are harder to appropriately update with new evidence.

A gem cannot be polished without friction, nor a man perfected without trials.
— *Seneca*

It is crucial that we come to view failure appropriately. We must see failures as a necessary part of life. We must recognize that failing at something now or in the past does not mean we will fail at it forever. We must recognize that failing in one area does not mean that we will fail in other areas. But most importantly, we must fully believe that failure has benefits. We must believe that failures can help us develop by forcing us to confront reality and determine how things really work. If we view failure appropriately, we are less likely to let our pride get in the way of learning the lessons it has to teach. And we are less likely to despair of our ability to accomplish great things because we could not accomplish them right away.

It is not just failures that help us learn and develop. We also learn from struggles and obstacles that we overcome. If everything always went our way and we did not have to make effort to get what we want, we would not have as much incentive to improve ourselves or learn how things work. Like failure, struggles and obstacles we encounter force us to learn. We should see them as opportunities to develop our minds and improve our understanding of the world. When anything is upsetting us, we must remember that there is a lesson to be learned, even if the result is simply our coming to better terms with a certain unpleasant truth about the world.

The most important single ingredient in the formula of success is knowing how to get along with people.
— Theodore Roosevelt

No matter how successful we are in some areas, we will not be successful overall without emotional intelligence—knowing how to get along with and influence other people and knowing how to control our emotions. We must not believe that we can focus on acquiring skills or achieving goals and neglect emotional intelligence. With emotional intelligence, we can more easily get others to help us accomplish our goals. Emotional intelligence will also help us avoid obstacles that others would otherwise put in our paths. We have the most control over ourselves, but done right, we can influence others positively. We must recognize fully that influencing others is both possible and extremely important for us to do.

Regarding influencing others, there is a lot for us to consider:

- There are many, many things we must know to master emotional intelligence, but one of the most powerful methods for getting along with and influencing people is simple. This method is to demonstrate to other people that we like them. And the best way to convince others that we like them is to not just appear to like them but to actually like them, which we can often achieve by focusing on their best and most likable qualities and on what we can learn from them. Not only will liking others make us more influential to them, it will also help ensure that we treat them the right way. This is important, for, in the long run, influencing others inappropriately is not in anyone's interest, including our own.

- Mastering our emotions—to the extent we can—must be a top priority for us. Without mastery of emotions, we cannot master emotional intelligence. Letting our judgment be overly clouded by emotions can lead us to quick actions before we fully consider their long-term consequences. These long-term consequences can include others growing to dislike us or be less influenced by us.

- We should not worry excessively about finding the perfect time or perfect wording to communicate certain things. For example, we must find time to show our love and appreciation of friends, family, colleagues whether it's the absolute best time and place or not. Similarly, we must find time to apologize for indiscretions, whether the timing or delivery is a little awkward or not. We must be careful about waiting for perfect conditions before we take important actions. Perfect conditions may never come, but the pain caused by not taking enough important actions certainly will.

- Even after becoming very emotionally intelligent, we must be cautious of the envy of others. Even if we are doing everything else right, envy can destroy our influence. Moreover, it can cause others to take actions that directly harm us. When we are fortunate, we must do as the Spanish writer and philosopher Baltasar Gracián once recommended: "Do not flaunt your good fortune." But even silent success can spark envy, so we must do more. We must be willing to be vulnerable occasionally, admitting to negative emotions we feel, faults we possess, and failures we have endured. Not doing so can eventually result in enemies for us. In many cases, these enemies will not be obvious—until it is too late.

- When it comes to how to get along with and influence others, we should be very careful about ever assuming that anyone operates completely without emotion. No one is so intelligent, so logical, or so wise that we can disregard the tenets of emotional intelligence in our interactions with them.

- We must be willing to have difficult conversations when necessary. In many cases, our problem is not so much being able to influence and get along with others as it is overcoming our aversion to the potential awkwardness that may result in asking others to do something we want them to do. This aversion can keep us from making simple requests that would yield great benefits for us. We should not be overly aggressive or demanding, but we should work to be assertive regarding important matters.

The difficulty is to try and teach the multitude that something can be true and untrue at the same time.
— Arthur Schopenhauer

The world is less black and white than most of us see it. We should use our rules, truths, and principles as guidelines but recognize that sometimes they do not apply. We must remember, a statement can be both true and untrue: true in certain circumstances and untrue in others. Rules have times they apply and times they do not. Taken to an extreme, nearly every rule is wrong. For example, consider the rule, "We must be self-reliant to live well." This has a lot of truth to it. In life, self-reliance is crucial. However, we should not aim to be 100% self-reliant, forgoing the help of others when it makes sense to get it. Our challenge is not only to know when to apply rules but also to know when not to apply them. We must not pass on good rules because they have exceptions to them, but we must work to learn the important exceptions.

As we encounter contradictions between truths, we should work to resolve them. But we should not do so by choosing our favorite truth as true and those that contradict it as false. Instead, we must determine when each truth applies and when it doesn't. For example, consider two truths: "absence makes the heart grow fonder" and "out of sight, out of mind." These truths contradict each other, but we should not resolve this contradiction by choosing one as superior. Instead, we might resolve the contradiction between them by thinking about when each applies. When it comes to these particular truths, the French aphorist and writer Francois de La Rochefoucauld did so beautifully when he wrote that "Absence diminishes mediocre passions and increases great ones, as the wind extinguishes candles and fans fires."

Truth, when not sought after, rarely comes to light.
— Oliver Wendell Holmes, Sr.

We can learn a lot from difficult experiences, failures, and harsh lessons from the School of Real Life, but the heights of wisdom and truth only come to those who also learn outside of situations in which they are forced to admit an error. The highest levels of truth only come to those who seek it. At best, only a modest amount will come to those who wait for it to be forced upon them.

The human brain is a complex organ with the wonderful power of enabling man to find reasons for continuing to believe whatever it is that he wants to believe.
— Voltaire

We must fully recognize that we and others will make endless errors even if earnestly seeking the truth. In order to minimize errors and correct them as quickly as possible, we must accept that we will make many of them. We must also pardon these errors. Otherwise, in an attempt to make ourselves feel better, we may rationalize that errors we make (real errors, not smart bets that do not work out) are not actually errors. We should use rationalization to allow ourselves to move on and not be bothered endlessly by mistakes we made in the past. But we must rationalize our mistakes the right way. We must recognize fully that in the past we made specific mistakes or missed specific opportunities. We can work to appreciate why we made these errors, acknowledging some of the constraints that made it difficult for us to see the truth or follow through with the right actions. This will help us feel better about our mistakes without needing to believe that they are not mistakes, making it easier to improve our behavior in the future.

Because a human being is so malleable, whatever one cultivates is what one becomes.
— Lao Tzu

Many of our qualities will stay fairly consistent throughout life, but many are quite alterable, particularly if we focus on changing them. We are too quick to think that things are more innate than they are, more genetic than they are. If we focus on something, practice it, and keep trying to improve it, we almost always can—often much more than we imagined we could when we began the process. We must rail against the popular belief that our qualities are more fixed than they actually are. Believing otherwise makes it more difficult to improve ourselves.

With self-discipline most anything is possible.
— Theodore Roosevelt

To accomplish big goals, we must have considerable self-discipline. We must be disciplined enough to put in the long hours a lofty goal requires and disciplined enough to avoid distractions that would cause us to lose focus and waste time and energy we need to allocate effectively. This can be painful if we do not view discipline the right way. As we develop self-discipline we must work to appreciate the benefits of being disciplined and not giving in to the tempting distractions around us. Eventually, once we have convinced ourselves adequately of the benefits, we can come to get a kind of pleasure from our discipline that helps us endure what we must.

It is notable that more discipline does not necessarily mean less overall freedom. We should not aim to be disciplined about everything, but we should have considerable discipline and structure in many areas in order to have greater freedom in others. We must determine what parts of our lives should have more freedom and which should have less. But when the situation calls for it, we must be flexible enough to give ourselves tremendous freedom in areas we normally do not.

As long as you live, keep learning how to live.
— Seneca

If we are to improve, we cannot develop a mindset where we believe that learning things means we are weak. As much as possible, we must always view ourselves, and the projects we engage in, as works in progress. Continuous personal growth is an important part of living well, and if we are able to embrace it, we will be amazed to find how much we can grow over time.

Faultless to a fault.
— Robert Browning

We should not "do our best" at everything we do. In many areas, we need to learn to be okay with doing a "good enough" job. Attempting to be too perfect in unimportant areas can harm our performance in important areas. Furthermore, insisting on perfection can stop us from trying at all when we believe our actions won't result in something perfect. We must care less about perfection, remembering that there is a lot of value in imperfect things: imperfect books, people, nations, apologies, displays of love and appreciation, and so on.

Logic: The art of thinking and reasoning in strict accordance with the limitations and incapacities of the human misunderstanding.
— Ambrose Bierce

If we do not have considerable real-world experience in an area, the logic and theories we try to apply to it are often lacking. Logic and theory only work if we know the important factors. If we try to use logic in a field we do not have much experience with, we might identify an important factor or two but miss others.

The former Secretary of Defense, Donald Rumsfeld, once noted that "There are known unknowns. That is to say, there are things that we know we don't know. But there are also unknown unknowns. There are things we don't know we don't know." We are far more likely to get blindsided by "unknown unknowns" in areas we do not have much experience with than in those we do have considerable experience with. Logic doesn't provide much protection from "unknown unknowns". At best it can help us take more precautions and be less confident in areas we have less experience with, as they are more likely to contain "unknown unknowns" that could hurt us.

Is there anyone so wise as to learn by the experience of others?
— Voltaire

We learn the most from our own mistakes, but it is of the utmost importance that we be able to learn from the mistakes that others make. As we consider these errors we must not be too dismissive of the possibility that we too could make them. We must not easily believe that we are too intelligent, too wise, too rational, or too even-keeled to need to take precautions to avoid the same errors.

In order to improve the mind, we ought less to learn, than to contemplate.
— René Descartes

When it comes to important rules and truths that we learn, we must remember that it is possible that we do not fully understand them. Frequently we may learn some of their applications but still miss many. For example, we might understand that failures and struggles help develop us but forget that they also do the same for our children.

It is also possible that we learn many of the applications of a rule but do not see some of its important exceptions. For example, we may understand that "patience is a virtue" but we may not understand that patience is not a virtue when it allows us to simply wait for something great to occur when we need to work to make it happen. The more deeply we think about what we experience, what others experience, the stories we hear, and the books we read, the less likely we are to miss helpful applications of and important exceptions to the rules and truths we learn from them.

The laws of circumstance are abolished by new circumstances.
— Napoleon Bonaparte

Even when we have seen lots of examples of a certain event always following another event, we must remember that things can be different in the future than we've ever seen before. Just because something has never happened before does not mean that it cannot happen. The circumstances that did not allow it to happen before might have changed. And if they have not changed yet, they could be susceptible to doing so in the future. We must strive for a fluid mind that does not overly rely on old rules.

There's a way to do it better—find it.
— Thomas Edison

There are two main ways we can accomplish more. We can work harder with the same methods and tools, or we can use new tools and methods that are potentially more productive. Working harder with the same methods and tools can increase our output, but this increase is linear at best—with 20% more effort yielding at most 20% more output. In contrast, better tools and methods can result in nonlinear improvements, potentially bringing tremendously more output for relatively little input. Working harder is often a temporary solution to increase productivity slightly. Working smarter is often the only way we can see sustained long-term improvements without harming other important aspects of our lives.

To work smarter, we must be ready to implement good ideas that others have. But this is insufficient. We must also be ready to be creative ourselves, improving upon the way things are currently done. The exact situations we encounter might never have been seen before, and others will not always be able to give us solutions to our problems.

As we work to increase our creativity, there is a lot for us to consider:

- We must recognize that to a large degree, creativity is a skill that can be developed. We must not think of ourselves as someone who isn't creative or cannot be.

- We should sometimes stop to ask if there are better ways to accomplish our goals. We should periodically engage in brainstorming better tools and methods to accomplish our goals. We should be willing to engage in trial and error to find better tools and methods. If we have an idea that seems like it could work but we aren't sure about it, we might consider experimenting with it. We must not be excessively afraid of being wrong. If the cost is low enough and the potential gain is big, it can make sense to try things we believe will not work on the off chance that we might be wrong and they do work—perhaps very well.

- We must not excessively stick to prior rules we or others have developed. We should use them as guidelines, but we must not be married to them. Many rules can constrain our creative talents in ways we should not allow.

- Many creative breakthroughs have come through having an unusual combination of knowledge of multiple fields. We can hope to grasp more of this creativity by learning more about the world. We should cultivate curiosity. When we encounter something that seems interesting and important, we might seek more information about it. We should occasionally read some nonfiction books on topics we would not normally choose. We should try new things periodically.

- We must cultivate being okay with not knowing the *complete* answer to, well, almost any question. This will help us to not jump to conclusions, giving us more chance to let more complete, more accurate answers come to us eventually.

It is better to be good than to be original.
— Ludwig Mies van der Rohe

We should look for the best ways to do things, whether they are old or new ideas. We must not worry so much about being original, as this can cause us to miss out on ideas that are old, but great. We should focus more on being effective than on being original.

Though men pride themselves on their great actions, often they are not the result of any great design, but of chance.
— Francois de La Rochefoucauld

Good luck is something we couldn't have reasonably fully predicted or controlled that helps us. Success usually requires intelligence, skill, and tenacity. These are important factors, but so is luck. Some level of luck—or at least not being unlucky—is almost always involved in achievements that truly stand out. With such achievements, there is nearly always some "right place, right time" involved that was impossible to fully know or predict in advance. Even if we can almost completely explain how we accomplished something great, so that there is little unexplained randomness, there may still have been luck involved in us getting to the place where we knew how to accomplish it. If we do not accept that there was *some* luck involved in much of the good that has come into our lives, we will not be grateful enough for it and we will not appreciate it in every way that we could.

On the other hand, while luck is nearly always a factor, we should not take it too far. We must not overvalue the role of luck in our lives and the lives of others. Great successes usually involve some good luck, but they also usually require considerable effort, persistence, and skill. We should be careful about believing that luck is more important than it is or that other factors are less important than they are. This is important to remember as we consider the accomplishments of others. It can be easy for us to write off their big achievements as "lucky," but this can prevent us from learning anything from their successes—and there's nearly always something for us to learn. It can also be very tempting to blame our own bad luck for our inability to accomplish goals. Doing this to excess can prevent us from taking enough ownership and making changes we are able to make to improve our lives.

As long as a man stands in his own way, everything seems to be in his way.
— Ralph Waldo Emerson

There are things we can't do much or anything about, but we often think we can do less than we can do. We must not accept that we do not have much power, blaming everything except ourselves for our inability to meet our goals. Blaming genetics is a crutch. Blaming human nature is a crutch. Blaming the foolishness of others is a crutch. There is some truth to the blame we lay on such things, but we can't stop there—not if we are to improve. We must worry less about what is fair. We must focus more on what we can do. It's much easier to change ourselves than the rest of the world. We must come to view our main obstacle in accomplishing great things as our failure to take enough personal responsibility. To be as productive as possible, we must keep learning better and better what is within our control at the same time that we accept more and more responsibility for these things.

We win half the battle when we make up our minds to take the world as we find it, including the thorns.
— Orison Marden

We will not be as happy or as wise as we could be until we accept the world the way it is, including its worst parts. We should not pretend that very bad things don't happen. We must accept hard truths about the world—how cruel and unfair it can be, how much pain there is for many of its inhabitants. Not doing so makes us unprepared for tragedies, both in avoiding them where we can and in recovering from them where we must.

As we consider things, we should not be quick to pass moral judgments like "good" or "bad" on them. These labels frequently oversimplify and can make us miss other important aspects these things have. We should spend more time concerned with what the world is rather than what it should be. We should spend more time concerned with what people do rather than on what they should do. This will help us understand people and the world a little better and will improve our responses to what we encounter in life.

We should aim to see things as they are. Not better than they are. Not worse than they are. We should believe that amazing things are possible but not necessarily that they are likely. We should believe that we and others are capable of enormous accomplishment and change but not that this is a given or that it won't take incredible effort in many cases.

Ah! If you only knew the peace there is in an accepted sorrow.
— Madame Jeanne Guyon

We are capable of overcoming so many misfortunes, but we often let things torment us far more than they have to, harming our happiness and our personal growth. When bad things happen, we should not fight being initially upset. When tragedies befall us, we should not try to avoid grieving. But in many cases, we should try to swallow the misfortune, accepting it and not stewing on it endlessly.

Forgiving others and releasing bitterness is a choice we make. In some cases, as we are reminded of upsetting things, we may have to repeatedly make this choice. We must also keep in mind that we can convince ourselves that we aren't bitter about certain things when we actually are. We must uncover such things so that we can work to move beyond them.

Everyone needs a sense of shame, but no one needs to feel ashamed.
— Friedrich Nietzsche

To correct ourselves, we must be able to recognize our errors, but we should not get hung up on them. Some shame can help us make positive changes for the future, but when we are ashamed for lengthy periods of time, it is counterproductive. We need to focus much more on what can be done going forward and much less on how we *could* have done things differently. If we cannot love ourselves for what we are or what we have done, we must get on a path toward significant positive change and love ourselves for doing that.

Be not a slave of your own past.
— Ralph Waldo Emerson

Making important corrections in our behavior is crucial, but there are many things that make it difficult to make these needed corrections. One such thing is our incredible ability to rationalize our bad behavior, coming to see it as acceptable or even good. This makes it easier for us to continue bad behavior. Something else that keeps us from making corrections is our drive to be consistent. If we see ourselves behaving a certain way, we tend to believe that we are the type of person that behaves that way and are more likely to keep behaving similarly. Understanding how strong rationalization and consistency are, the novelist and poet Mary Anne Evans (known by her pen name George Eliot) once noted that "Our deeds determine us, as much as we determine our deeds." But it doesn't have to be that way. We must fight vigorously against the tendency to rationalize our bad behavior. We must fight vigorously against believing that we are a certain type of person who always behaves a certain type of way, as this can keep us from acting differently when it will yield us better results. We must never settle for foolish consistencies.

When it comes to ourselves, it's important to recognize that we have a tremendous capacity for change. We must never let ourselves believe that living a certain way in the past means that we cannot live differently in the future, whether or not others believe we can change.

When it comes to others, we should be reasonably open to the possibility that those who made mistakes in the past will learn from them. But we should not be foolish. Belief in the human capacity for change should be tempered by the knowledge that many negative qualities are very hard to change and will never change for many people. Although significant positive change in others may be too rare, as we interact with people, we must remember that showing them that we believe in their ability to improve can help them to actually change in important ways.

A precondition for reading good books is not reading bad ones: for life is short.
— Arthur Schopenhauer

Being excessively idle and not working hard enough is a problem, but working hard on the wrong things is often a bigger problem. To accomplish what is truly important will take lots of our time...time we won't have if we are doing too many unimportant things. To be more productive, one strategy is to fill as much of our free time as possible with activity. But a better strategy is removing unproductive activities so that we can focus more on the important ones.

We can't just do our best. We have to do our best at the right things. And we have to do our best to find out what the right things are!

The greatest thing in the world is to know how to belong to oneself.
— Michel de Montaigne

There are certain qualities and knowledge that everyone should seek. There are other qualities and knowledge that we should only seek based on our own unique background, interests, and strengths. The answer to the question "How do I live well?" varies a lot from person to person.

As we work to discover how to live well we should keep the following in mind:

- We should not be overly afraid to stand out from others or be different. The best success often comes not from working very hard on the goals and methods of others but through finding better methods to achieve our goals or by finding better goals entirely.

- We are all influenced by other people. It is silly to think that any of us are not. And we *should* be influenced by them in many ways. However, we should work to differentiate between good and bad influence. Most of us should work to reduce our need for approval from others so that we can think more clearly and avoid bad influence. We must also work to not put ourselves in positions in which we are repeatedly exposed to societal absurdities and pressures that will negatively influence us no matter how resolved we are to not let them.

- We must not try to please everyone, but we should try to get along with others when possible. We should be willing to offend others, but we should not do so needlessly! We must be able to stand up for what is important, but we should not usually have to aggressively contradict others when we disagree with them.

- Our uniqueness may lead us to great results, but it won't always get us the credit we deserve. Many may resent that we did things outside of normal conventions, even if our doing things differently led to success. We must mentally prepare for this in advance. It won't make it easy, but it will soften the eventual blow.

Stop competing with others and start competing with yourself.
— Unknown

We must recognize that other people have different advantages and disadvantages and start from different places than us. Not being able to beat someone at a certain activity at a certain point may not say much about our ultimate capability in the activity or our capability in other pursuits.

Most of us should compare ourselves less to others. Excessive comparison to others leads to foolish competition with others. Wanting to keep up with or beat others can cause us to put too much effort into unimportant areas. We should worry less about coming out on top of many of the activities we are defaulted into competing in, and we should worry more about succeeding at the right activities.

Even if we are focusing on worthy goals, we must be careful. Too frequently, competition can leave us stressed and unwilling to take a step backward to take two steps forward, either by taking the time to learn better ways to do things or creatively finding them ourselves. We must work hard to not let competition fixate us on the short-term, making us miss what could deliver us the greatest long-term success.

Every increased possession loads us with a new weariness.
—John Ruskin

Possessions take money to buy. They take up space. They take time, effort, and money to maintain. We can feel bad for not using them more than we do. Almost every possession has potential benefits, but the problem for many possessions is that we do not benefit from them much of the time. Reducing possessions generally gives us more flexibility, more time, and more money, which gives us more freedom and more potential for quality experiences.

We must understand that we often do not need to own things in order to enjoy them. We don't have to own artwork to appreciate it. We don't need to own a pool to swim at one we are a member of. We don't need to own many acres of land to enjoy many acres of land at a local park. In fact, in many cases, we can enjoy things more without owning them because we are free of the burdens their ownership would bring us.

To do great work, a man must be very idle as well as very industrious.
— Samuel Butler

We can become so busy accomplishing goals that we often don't engage in enough reflection to determine if we're accomplishing the right ones. Even if we are working toward the right goals, we often don't take enough time to consider if we are tackling these goals in the best ways. We should not demand constant output from ourselves, as this can prevent us from entering some of our most productive states of mind— in which we aren't just taking action but are selecting the best actions to take.

We must take breaks from work. Some breaks should come in the form of relaxation, during which we do not directly work on solving problems. We must make sure that such breaks do not always involve activities that require a level of mental focus that leaves our unconscious mind unable to help solve important problems in our lives. As the Chinese philosopher and writer, Lao Tzu noted, "Doing nothing is better than being busy doing nothing." Other breaks from work should be used to directly ask and answer important questions such as "Are there better ways to accomplish the goals we have?" or "Are there better goals to take on?"

A reasonable amount of breaks from work makes us more productive, but this is not the only reason we should take breaks. Without adequate breaks, life becomes exponentially more difficult. It becomes much less enjoyable. Without adequate breaks, our health can suffer greatly, both mentally and physically.

We should endeavor to see breaks as necessary so that we take enough of them. If we have trouble stopping hard work, we may need to force ourselves to take breaks by scheduling them into our days.

If there is something to pardon in everything, there is also something to condemn.
— Friedrich Nietzsche

There are pros and cons to everything. As we try to choose amongst options, we should look for opportunity in seemingly negative things and drawbacks in seemingly positive things so they can be weighed appropriately and allow us to make better decisions. If we are forced down a path we for which we did not plan, we should seek to maximize the opportunities of this path. Baltasar Gracián once wrote that "Many things cause pain that would cause pleasure if you regarded their advantages." The point here is not that bad things are actually good—although sometimes they are. The point is that we will be happier and more productive if we focus on the good parts of seemingly bad things that befall us. We should be grateful for the growth and learning we get from solving difficult problems and overcoming obstacles. We should be grateful that hard times have made us more appreciative of better times to come.

The essayist and poet Ralph Waldo Emerson once observed that "Our strength grows out of our weakness." An introvert can use the increased alone time their "weakness" of introversion brings to focus on and master the field of their choice. Someone who is physically disabled can use this "weakness" to spend more time and energy to improve their mental, emotional, or spiritual lives. Our weaknesses can lead us to great strength, but this is not automatic. To maximize the opportunity for strengths to grow from these weaknesses, we must not feel sorry for ourselves, and we must focus on what we can do rather than on what we cannot do.

For age is opportunity no less Than youth itself, though in another dress, And as the evening twilight fades away The sky is filled with stars invisible by day.
— Henry Wadsworth Longfellow

We should not see aging as a purely bad thing—it's not. There are pros and cons to all stages of life, and we must not exaggerate the cons or downplay the pros to old age. We should be careful about believing that we cannot or should not do certain activities as we get older. We must work to not believe that aging constrains us more than it does. We are capable of changing, improving, and learning well into old age, and we must work hard to make sure that we do so. Doing so will make us happier and perhaps even lead us to accomplish different and greater things than we could have in our youth.

Our life is what our thoughts make it.
— *Marcus Aurelius*

Our beliefs about things often matter much more to our happiness (or unhappiness) than the things themselves. The right beliefs can make us grateful for the good in our lives—the way that we should be. The right beliefs can help us appreciate the good aspects of bad things—to the extent possible. At a minimum, the right beliefs can help us to not view negative things as worse than they are.

There is much we should consider regarding how our thoughts affect our lives:

- Adopting the right beliefs can help us to avoid suffering. Suffering usually requires us to believe that we will have a significant amount of pain in the future. In many cases, this is because we have not properly evaluated things. Perhaps we have exaggerated the impact or risk of negative things we face. Perhaps we have missed the advantages that accompany disadvantages (for example, the personal growth we get from overcoming struggles in life). Significant suffering usually requires us to believe a devastating story—such as "This will ruin my life" or "This is hopeless." If we find ourselves suffering, we need to examine the stories we believe and work to improve them. When we notice a story is causing us pain, we must look for specific logical flaws in it and counter them. For example, if our story ends with "This will ruin my life," we would do well to remember that there are few things that can truly ruin our lives if we are determined not to let them. But it is not just correcting logical flaws like this that is helpful. We must also balance negative implications of our stories with positive—but equally valid—implications. For example, we might note that we failed to accomplish a goal and that we must try again while also recognizing that we now are better prepared to exceed our original goal.

- Many of us accumulate a whole series of unresolved issues that continuously flow throughout our unconscious, and make us more unhappy and anxious than they have to. To best combat these stressors, we must bring them to the forefront where our conscious mind can work to counteract them. It is useful to periodically list out everything that could potentially be bothering us, and then let the wisest parts of us weigh in on how to remedy them or at least how to feel better about them. We should dig deep with this list, being careful not to leave things off it that we feel we should not allow ourselves to be bothered by, because often these things bother us more than we like to admit.

- Just as what we think matters, so does what we say—to ourselves and to others. If we want to change the way we think and feel about something, we need to change the way we talk about it, too. Continuously complaining or excessively talking about problems can make them more bothersome than they have to be.

- Although our beliefs matter a lot, they are not everything. We cannot remove all feelings of stress or fear by believing they are not productive or necessary to feel. We also cannot make ourselves feel totally content while we are enduring significant physical pain. As William Shakespeare put it, "There was never yet a philosopher who could endure a toothache patiently." We must not come to believe that all our negative feelings come from our inability to direct our thoughts appropriately.

One resolution I have made, and try to always keep, is this: "to rise above the little things."
— John Burroughs

If we let truly little things (a spilled drink, a long line at the store, a restaurant out of a menu item, etc.) bother us much at all, our moods will constantly be taking a turn for the worse, as life is completely packed with potential small annoyances and irritations. We will never stop all little things from bothering us some, but living well requires us to be barely bothered at all by most small things.

We must work to not be very bothered by foolish opinions or whims of others. We must work to not be very bothered by silly things others do. Generally, we must view these as little things. It is rare that it makes sense to fight hard to change or oppose human stupidity. We should in many ways resign ourselves to having to face lots of foolishness from others without being overly bothered by it, perhaps even finding a small measure of humor or pleasure in it where possible.

The mind is like a river; upon its waters thoughts float through in a constant procession every conscious moment. It is a narrow river, however, and you stand on a bridge over it and can stop and turn back any thought that comes along, and they can only come single file, one at a time. The art of contentment is to let no thought pass that is going to disturb you.
— Frank Crane

It has been said that we should not believe everything we think, and we absolutely should not. Furthermore, we should not be disappointed with ourselves for not preventing *initial* thoughts and feelings that are unproductive. As we experience thoughts and feelings we should work to determine if they are productive. If they are, we should promote them. If they are not, we should work to correct them. When we notice we are engaging in overly negative thinking, we should direct our thoughts to something more helpful. Learning to quickly stop downward spirals of one negative thought leading to another is one of the most effective ways to improve our moods.

If you scramble about in search of inner peace, you will lose your inner peace.
— Lao Tzu

No one is always happy. We aren't meant to be happy all the time. It is natural to have some stress and anxiety and depression. Not only is it natural, it can also have benefits. For example, anxiety can help ensure that we work hard and focus enough to accomplish an important goal. Even when we are experiencing unhelpful stress, it is not always useful to take much action to fight it. Stress often has to run its course to some degree. Fighting it can make it much worse than it would otherwise be.

It's good to keep in mind that life can be enjoyed even while we are experiencing some level of worry, stress, anxiety, and so on. We must not believe that we need to get our stress level to zero before we can enjoy life.

Gratitude is not only the greatest of virtues, but the parent of all others.
— Marcus Cicero

It is tremendously important that we foster gratitude. Gratitude makes us happier by helping us focus on the good in our lives. Gratitude makes us less desperate to make changes to our lives, and therefore less impatient and less prone to foolish short-term thinking. Furthermore, having significant gratitude makes it difficult for us to be arrogant or prideful to our detriment.

Generally, we aren't grateful enough for what we have accomplished or what we have experienced or what we currently have. We readily see what we have not yet accomplished, have not experienced, or don't currently have. Fixating on things we do not have and believing that they are required to make us happy is a surefire way of staying unhappy. We should work hard to remember the good we have in our lives now and the good we have had in the past. We must periodically take the time to appreciate what we have accomplished rather than focusing on what we have not yet accomplished.

It's not just the exceptionally good things that we should appreciate. Having gratefulness for common or simple things is important. We should be grateful for our basic needs being met. We should be grateful for tragedies not befalling us. As the clergyman and social reformer, Henry Ward Beecher put it, "The art of being happy lies in the power of extracting happiness from common things."

We can't just decide to be grateful once and be grateful effortlessly from there on out. Gratefulness must be practiced. After much practice, it becomes easier to be grateful, but for most of us, it will always take some effort. Without enough effort, it is easy to fall back into ungrateful ways. To make sure we are grateful enough, we must remind ourselves to be grateful on an almost daily basis.

Who is the happiest of men? He who values the merits of others, and in their pleasure takes joy, even as though 'twere his own.
— Johann Wolfgang von Goethe

There is something to learn from people who are successful at something, even those who are lacking in other ways. Our envy of another's success or good qualities can cause us to miss the lessons they have to teach us. When envious, we may make a logical error, believing that because a person has *some* negative qualities, they do not have anything worthwhile to teach us. We must be aware of and fight this tendency. If we work to admire rather than envy successful people, we can better emulate them.

Appreciating the good qualities of others helps us learn from them. It also makes us happier, and it makes our relationships better. The philosopher William James once noted that "The deepest principle in human nature is the craving to be appreciated." We all want to be appreciated for the contributions we make, for the skills we have developed, for our good qualities, and so forth. Not showing adequate appreciation to others can cause strife in our relationships.

To be as happy and productive as we can be, we cannot just appreciate the good qualities of others. We must also work to enjoy good things that happen to others—even good fortune they did little to earn.

Whether happiness may come or not, one should try to prepare one's self to do without it.
— Mary Ann Evans (known by her pen name George Eliot)

Some people are happier than others, and it would be great for us to be amongst the happiest people. But even under ideal circumstances, this may not be in the cards for us. We can be happier by preparing ourselves to do without the highest levels of happiness. This means not striving so hard for happiness and not beating ourselves up for not feeling as happy as we think we should.

Be master of thy anger.
— Periander of Corinth

The Chinese teacher and philosopher Confucius once said, "When anger rises think of the consequences." As Confucius knew, angry actions and speech can cause irreparable harm.

There is much we should consider regarding anger:

- As a rule, we should not take action while angry, giving ourselves time to calm down and review all our options first.

- We must learn to not take things personally. By not taking things personally, we won't get angry nearly as often, and we will think more clearly. Even when someone clearly has ill intent toward us, and we should, in a sense, take their words or actions personally, we should take a step back and think about the bigger picture. With our larger goals in mind, we can make better decisions.

- Part of mastering anger is not ever thinking we are immune to taking angry actions. Sometimes it's best to avoid situations that could make us angry. We cannot always avoid things that anger us, but when we find ourselves in a situation that is making us angry, we should be prepared to walk away before we take foolish actions.

- Even if our anger does not cause us to take foolish actions, we should be careful not to let ourselves feel intense anger for long periods of time. We can dislike something, but we should avoid intense anger, as it kills our happiness.

- *Very* controlled displays of anger can occasionally be helpful. It's rare, but we should give ourselves the flexibility to show anger when the right situation arises.

A man who suffers before it is necessary, suffers more than is necessary.
— Seneca

We suffer excessively from fear when we fear things we cannot control. For example, we may fear bad things that could happen to us such as losing our job, getting sick, or dying. We can work to prevent these things to some degree, but excessively fearing them, beyond the point it helps us take reasonable steps to prevent them or prepare for them, causes us needless suffering.

There are many things in life that are out of our control. It does us no good to worry about these things. Other things in life are at least somewhat within our control. While *worrying* about what is under our control rarely makes much sense either, thinking ahead about it can be productive. Thinking ahead can help us determine the best actions we can take to solve problems we know are coming. Although there are benefits to thinking ahead, doing so excessively can cause us to suffer more than we should as we repeatedly review stressful problems. We have to watch for where our thinking ahead and planning cease to be helpful. In such cases, we have to be disciplined about finding ways to move on to more productive things. For example, with certain problems, after planning our next step, it may be prudent not to think about the problem again until we arrive at the stage of action.

The only thing we have to fear is fear itself.
— Franklin D. Roosevelt

Fear can hold us back by keeping us from taking smart risks in our lives. We might fear to make a big life change, such as leaving a dead-end job or leaving a bad relationship, exaggerating the potential negative outcomes. It's important to be aware of the potential downsides to actions we may take, but we must also be aware of the downsides of inaction. In the long run, not taking reasonable risks will usually hurt us more than errors we may make in trying to change our lives for the better. Perhaps what we should fear the most in life is stagnating and ceasing to improve because we are too afraid to make important changes.

An ounce of prevention is worth a pound of cure.
— Benjamin Franklin

We have huge limitations on our ability to predict the future, but it is necessary to look several steps ahead, thinking about the potential consequences of our actions. Many negative situations are easier to prevent than to overcome. We need to think about the secondary effects of our actions. In other words, we must not take actions to accomplish one goal without considering how these actions will impact other important goals that we have. We must never allow our success at one goal to cause us failure in more important goals.

When it comes to our goals, we must think ahead. We must ask ourselves some important questions. What would happen if we accomplished our current goals? How would it feel? What would our next goal be? This simple line of questioning may help us uncover long in advance if our goals are worthwhile. If we find that they are not, we can change course before too much damage is done.

That gain should never be regarded highly which leadeth to loss. On the other hand, that loss even should be regarded highly which would bring on gain.
— The Mahabharata (ancient Indian epic)

We must recognize that it's not worth fighting every battle that we could win. Declining the right battles allows us to pursue more productive ventures, avoid collateral damage, and gain peace of mind.

We must be careful about succeeding at any single goal that causes harm to other important goals. We must become very aware of pyrrhic victories—victories whose gains are not worth it because they come at too high of a cost—and we must work to utterly detest them. We shouldn't be afraid to look stupid if looking stupid is outweighed by a greater gain. Similarly, we should not be afraid to look weak, appear cowardly, or have any attribute typically seen as negative if this is worth it in a particular situation, all things considered.

Pride, the never-failing vice of fools.
— Alexander Pope

We must be forever ready to swallow our pride and humble ourselves as it is frequently necessary. Excessive pride and ego make it difficult to admit and correct faults. Pride can cause us to fight battles that are clearly at the expense of the overall war. Pride can lead us to take foolish actions to prove our worth. It can lead us to overreact to someone who has injured our pride in some way. Furthermore, too much ego can cause us to miss out on good ideas that we have unfairly evaluated because we did not come up with them ourselves.

Very related to pride is stubbornness. There are times when we should be nearly certain we are right, but we have to be careful about adopting such a position without enough consideration to determine that this truly makes sense. We must do as Baltasar Gracián advised and "Never do something out of stubbornness, only out of attentive reflection."

First say to yourself what you would be; and then do what you have to do.
— Epictetus

Having goals is crucial. Goals can help focus our attention on what is important and direct us to concrete, productive actions. But having goals does not automatically make us more productive. We have to know how to create good goals and how to prioritize them, and we have to know when to give up goals and when to redouble our efforts to achieve them. And we must not be overly focused on goals. Sometimes our only goals should be to enjoy what we are experiencing and to be open to whatever lessons it might teach us.

Giving up doesn't always mean you are weak. Sometimes it means you are strong enough to let go.
— Unknown

While we must be cautious about giving up on good goals, we must recognize that it is not necessarily a fault to do so—plenty of times, it is a strength. We should be flexible with our goals, and we must not, out of slavish adherence to a rule, finish things when our time would be better spent elsewhere. We must fully recognize that one of our perennial goals should be finding even better goals.

It is a bad plan that admits of no modification.
— Publilius Syrus

We must create goals, but we also must create plans to reach our goals. Without plans, we may have dreams that we never take enough action to achieve. As the writer and poet Antoine de Saint-Exupery noted, "A goal without a plan is just a wish." Plans are crucial, but not just any plan will do—we must plan intelligently. We must understand that our plans should not depend on everything going according to plan. We must make contingency plans. As we plan, we must prepare for the possibility of being wrong about some of the assumptions we made. When possible, we should have decent alternatives for important parts of our plan. We must be flexible enough to not let overly strict adherence to our plan interfere with reaching our goal.

In great attempts it is glorious even to fail.
— Cassius Longinus

We must not shy away from big goals and dreams. To achieve big, we almost have to dream big. If we fail while trying to accomplish something great, we may still accomplish something impressive in the process, or we may be set up to eventually achieve even greater things than we have thus far failed to accomplish. We must not stop dreaming big in general because a certain big dream couldn't be fulfilled.

We should dream big, but we must be cautious about committing considerable resources to interesting ideas that pop into our heads without enough vetting. We might set a relatively low bar for beginning to get information on a topic or spending a smaller amount of time and resources pursuing something while setting a much higher bar for putting significant time and effort into something. If an idea is interesting enough, it might warrant some research. If after this research it looks promising, it might warrant still further research. If it still looks good afterwards, we might then commit further time and resources to it. But only after we have seen enough evidence of value should we risk *significant* time and resources. We have to take risks in life, but they should be justifiable.

Perpetual devotion to what a man calls his business is only to be sustained by perpetual neglect of many other things.
— Robert Louis Stevenson

Work is an important part of life, but it is just that—a part. Too much time spent working means too little time spent doing other important things.

If we don't schedule priorities they can get overtaken by urgent-seeming, but less important things. We must set aside time to begin important things, or else we may never begin them. We must set aside time to review where we are and where we are going. We must set aside time for learning and self-development. We must set aside time to be with the people we love. We must set aside time for breaks.

Patience is the companion of wisdom.
— Saint Augustine

The inventor Thomas Edison once noted, "Everything comes to him who hustles while he waits." As Edison implies, we can't just wait for great things to happen; we have to make them happen. As we patiently work to accomplish goals, we must continuously evaluate our actions to make sure we are doing the right things and aren't awaiting something that won't happen. Patience is a virtue, except when it prevents us from taking the right actions.

We must not expect ourselves to accomplish great things without great effort and lots of time. If we are resolved to accomplish great things and are moving in a direction to do so, we should be patient. We must not take excessive risks or foolish shortcuts because we are impatient or trying to fit things into some short and arbitrary timeframe. Not only is extreme pressure to quickly succeed at a goal often counterproductive for achieving that particular goal, it can also make us enjoy life less.

We must recognize that in life, we will all feel defeated at times. There will be misfortunes and unpleasant circumstances we must endure. During such times, we must be patient, striving to keep our eye on the big picture. If we have to give up on a specific goal, we should not let this stop us from dreaming big in general. If we don't give up on achieving big things, if we continue to learn and grow, we will be better prepared to capitalize on future opportunities. When necessary we must do as the poet Virgil once advised, "Persevere and preserve yourself for better circumstances."

Judge each day not by the harvest you reap but by the seeds you plant.
— Robert Louis Stevenson

Concrete, obvious benefits to our hard work and learning usually do not come immediately. We must become comfortable with the relationship between effort and results, which is often nonlinear. We must remember that we can put forth a lot of effort with few results, followed by a little more effort with huge results. If we are moving in the right direction, breakthroughs will eventually come.

For countless people there is only one remedy: the catastrophe.
— Christian Morgenstern

Reacting to obvious problems in our lives and making changes to solve them will result in improvements over time. Acting proactively, without a pressing need to change, instead of reacting, will allow us to change more frequently and see greater improvements over time. We must not require what most people would label a catastrophe to change. We must recognize the crisis of not changing proactively!

As we work to change more proactively, we should keep some things in mind:

- Change can be painful, and this often keeps us from being proactive enough about it. But if we have a good attitude about change and dive into it, it is often much less painful than we thought it would be. Humans are extremely adaptable.

- We must not expect good changes to be better in every possible way. We must expect some downsides. We must seek changes that are better overall, not better in every way.

- While implementing a positive change, we may be less productive for a time than we would have been without doing so. However, we have to be willing to take a step backward to go two steps forward. In fact, in many cases, we must be willing to accept an up-front cost without knowing for sure if it will result in any benefits at all. In other words, we must be willing to go a step backward to *attempt* to go two steps (or many more) forward. The essayist and poet Ralph Waldo Emerson once noted, "All life is an experiment. The more experiments you make the better." Emerson understood that trial and error is a necessary part of living well. It can result in spectacular finds.

Great things are done by a series of small things brought together.
— Vincent Van Gogh

Making numerous small improvements can add up tremendously over time. We must not foolishly pass on incremental improvements because we are too impatient or looking for a silver bullet. We must give adequate credit to solving little parts of big problems. Often big problems can only be tackled by dealing with smaller, more manageable parts. We must remember to be grateful for our little victories in life, and for the small things we learn.

Seemingly small things that get repeated over and over can actually be big things. We should consider the cost and benefit of implementing little changes to our routines or processes. Many such changes have very low cost compared to their benefit. For example, it may take a little up-front work to acquire a good habit, but once it's been set up, it might not take much effort to continue it and reap its benefits indefinitely.

The beginning of wisdom is the definition of the terms.
— Socrates

Careless use and interpretation of language can cause us to make errors. We must think more about the important words and phrases we and others use and do our best to define them. What is wisdom? What is love? What does it mean to live well? What does it mean to treat others well? And what do these things *not* mean?

When we describe anything in our lives, we should be careful about rough descriptions when something more precise is helpful. Instead of telling ourselves that we are "not good at public speaking," we might be a bit more precise and say that we are "not good at public speaking yet, but could be much better with practice." This increased precision gives us more opportunity to improve ourselves. As another example, when we declare that a person is successful, we might make sure to indicate how specifically they are successful and perhaps how specifically they are not successful. This can help us ensure that we emulate their best qualities and avoid inadvertently emulating their worst qualities.

We must also not forget that describing something with negative language can make us miss its good parts. And describing something with positive language can make us miss its bad parts.

To say that man is made up of strength and weakness, of insight and blindness, of pettiness and grandeur, is not to draw up an indictment against him: it is to define him.
— Denis Diderot

We simplify things, believing that we and others are good, bad, hardworking, lazy, bold, timid, and so on. The truth is we aren't fully any of these things, nor are we fully their opposites. We can have good qualities in certain ways and have their opposites in other ways. For example, a person can be "lazy" when it comes to a job they dislike but hardworking when it comes to working on something they are passionate about. When something is described as having a certain quality, we need to consider how specifically it has that quality and understand that it may not have that quality in other aspects. Furthermore, as we encounter negative qualities in others, we should not forget that we often share them in some way or to some degree.

No one has ever learned fully to know themselves.
— Johann Wolfgang von Goethe

In order to know ourselves better than most people know themselves, we must understand that we cannot fully know ourselves or even come close to doing so. It's hard for us to know what would make us happy. It is hard for us to know exactly how we would feel or exactly what we would do in many situations. We must work to not be overly confident in our predictions about the world, including our own reactions to events. We have all surprised ourselves before, and we will all surprise ourselves again. We will surprise ourselves a little less by remembering this.

The true wisdom is to always be seasonable, and to change with a good grace in changing circumstances.
— Robert Louis Stevenson

In life, no one tactic is best in every situation. A variety of tactics are necessary for the variety of situations we can find ourselves in. Everyone is somewhat flexible with their tactics, but the ideal amount of flexibility is more than most people have. We must be ready to bend even our best rules when it makes sense to. We must also be ready to act contrary to our normal qualities, keeping in mind that even the best personal characteristics are not the best in every situation. Sometimes it makes sense for an outgoing person to be more reserved or a reserved person to be more outgoing. Sometimes it makes sense for a generous person to be more selfish. Sometimes it makes sense for an organized person to let a little mess into their lives. Sometimes it makes sense for a self-reliant person to get more help. The more intelligently flexible we are, the more effective we will be.

The wise may find in trifles light as atoms in the air, some useful lesson to enrich the mind.
— John Godfrey Saxe

We should seek quality experiences but make the most of poor ones. We have more opportunity to learn and grow from certain experiences, but we can learn from nearly everything if we try, including what we have repeated many times. There are many lessons to learn from most experiences, and we must not assume there is only one or are only a few.

It is not doing the thing we like to do, but liking the thing we have to do, that makes life blessed.
— Johann Wolfgang von Goethe

If we have to do something, we should try to enjoy it as much as we can. Similarly, if we have to be around certain people, it may make sense to try to like them as much as we can, or at least to work to appreciate the lessons we can learn from them. We may never be fully comfortable with difficult people or situations, but we should work to minimize the pain they can cause us. In working to like something more, it helps to focus on its benefits—and there are always some.

The highest reward for a person's toil is not what they get for it, but what they become by it.
— John Ruskin

Self-development and becoming wiser should always be top priorities for us. If we don't learn to live well, we may not thrive in even the best circumstances. If we do learn to live well, we can recover from some of the worst possible setbacks.

We cannot remain happy for long without making progress. We are wired to need to get better and better. We must not try to fight this, struggling to be happy without having to make progress. Instead, we must embrace making continuous improvements in our lives. But we must channel this need for progress appropriately by not just becoming better but becoming better in ways that truly matter.

*Human beings are born into this little span of life of which
the best thing is its friendships and intimacies, and soon
their places will know them no more, and yet they leave
their friendships and intimacies with no cultivation, to
grow as they will by the roadside, expecting them to "keep"
by force of inertia.*
— *William James*

We must recognize that we cannot become happy purely through pursuing the types of things typically thought to be in our self-interest. We must not think that we can achieve happiness without significant love of others and from others. We must never come to believe that we can live well without highly prioritizing the happiness, the hopes, and the dreams of our spouse or partner.

Relationships take work. We can't show our love, our appreciation, and how much we care at one point and believe this continues indefinitely without further demonstration. Good relationships can become easier, but we should never believe that they will become effortless.

Actions are often more important than words, but we must not neglect words. While we shouldn't expect others to show their love with words, we should be willing to do so ourselves. We should make our appreciation of loved ones obvious.

He who does not trust enough will not be trusted.
— Lao Tzu

Plenty of caution is warranted in our dealings with others. We must not trust others excessively, but we must not distrust them excessively either. Excessive distrust of others lowers our quality of life. It can cause us unneeded fear and worry and can harm our relationships with others. It can cause us to not seek needed help from others or make intelligent transactions with them.

If we show our distrust of someone to them, we can bring out their bad side. If we intelligently show them some trust—at least for matters of smaller importance—we can cause them to become better as they try to live up to our expectations of them.

We have to be able to risk allowing ourselves to love others and risk allowing them to love us back. Doing so opens us up to hurt, but we must recognize the greater risk of missing out on the love we could have had.

No one has ever properly understood me, I have never fully understood anyone; and no one understands anyone else.
— Johann Wolfgang Von Goethe

We should never expect others to fully appreciate all that we are or do. We should never expect others to fully understand all of our hopes, dreams, or interests. We should not expect others to fully understand our struggles or fears or constraints either. We should also not expect ourselves to fully understand these things about others, even those we know very well.

In many ways, we are all better than others will ever know, but we must not drive ourselves crazy trying to prove our worth or talents.

The truth is, everyone is going to hurt you. You just got to find the ones worth suffering for.
— Often attributed to Bob Marley

Good people are not good in every way and will make mistakes. They can and will hurt us at times. We must not search for anyone or anything without negatives. Instead, we must search for what is worth it overall, all things considered.

The essence of philosophy is that a man should so live that his happiness shall depend as little as possible on external things.
— Epictetus

We should work to make our happiness depend little on external things. Part of this is achieved through changing the way we think about things, for how we interpret them often matters more than the things themselves. However, we cannot fully control how we interpret—and therefore how we feel about—such external things. Because we can't just depend solely on mastering the way we interpret things, we should avoid exposure to certain things. This can include stressful jobs, excessive commitments, difficult people, and the like. We must stop making excuses for not avoiding such things. Although it is unclear if he said it, Albert Einstein is widely credited with stating that "Insanity is doing the same thing over and over again and expecting different results." This idea applies to certain annoyances in our lives. Expecting ourselves to not be repeatedly annoyed as we continually expose ourselves to them is a sort of insanity.

The aim of an argument or discussion should not be victory, but progress.
— *Joseph Joubert*

It is worth remembering that in most disagreements there is at least some truth to what both sides say, even if one of those sides is mostly wrong. We should not view arguments for or against something as all-or-nothing propositions; we can accept parts of an argument but reject other parts. Although it can be difficult, accepting parts of arguments we mostly oppose can lead us to much greater understanding.

To find fault is easy; to do better may be difficult.
— Plutarch

It is important to be able to recognize when something has drawbacks, but this recognition should be combined with further steps of deciding what parts of it are good, what parts could be improved if any, and if it's worth it overall after the costs of such improvements. Sometimes the best option has obvious drawbacks but is still the best overall. We should focus on finding better ways to do things and complain less about the way they are done now.

If evil be said of thee, and if it be true, correct thyself; if it be a lie, laugh at it.
— Epictetus

When we are criticized accurately, even if it is done poorly or meanly, we should not miss the opportunity to learn from it and improve. It can be especially difficult to respond appropriately when someone says something negative about us that contains both some truth and also some falseness or exaggeration, but we must work hard to do so.

We must be able to correct our faults, even if others detail them to us rudely. However, we should make it easier for others to correct their own faults by criticizing them in kinder, more effective ways.

You must accept the truth from whatever source it comes.
— Maimonides

It can be a major oversimplification to declare someone to be knowledgeable or ignorant without clarifying that this applies only to certain areas. Nearly everyone is skilled in a way that most others are not. We should always remember the words of Ralph Waldo Emerson: "Every man I meet is in some way my superior."

We should be prepared to learn what we can from everyone, ready to capitalize on the useful parts of what someone says or does. We must not miss truth because it is mixed with nontruth. We should discard what is not useful and seize what is.

We are all something, but none of us are everything.
— Blaise Pascal

Some self-sufficiency is crucial, but taking it too far is foolish. We must not adhere to some silly rule that we need to be totally self-sufficient. We must allow ourselves to learn from others, never believing that we must figure out how to do everything on our own. But this is not enough. We must recognize that in many cases, it is more beneficial to get others to perform certain tasks for us rather than getting them to help us do it ourselves. We cannot master all skills, and we should consider the massive opportunity cost of trying to do so. Even if we already know how to do something well, it can make sense to have someone else do it for us, as this can free us up to do something more important. We must be able to delegate and make intelligent use of the assistance of others.

Ask for advice. And then use your brain.
— Norwegian proverb

Accurate, rapid feedback about the effectiveness of our goals and our attempts to reach them is critical. Feedback helps us make needed corrections and improve. We must solicit feedback. We must ask specifically for criticism and ways to improve. To make sure we get the best feedback, we must make it easy for others to give it, encouraging it and never being angry receiving it. Of course, not all feedback will be helpful. We should use good feedback and throw away the bad, as long as we have given enough fair consideration to the feedback to determine that it is actually bad.

Know how to rely on yourself.
— Baltasar Gracián

Getting help from others is often required to succeed at something meaningful, but we cannot come to rely on anyone more than ourselves. We must cultivate a high level of self-reliance, believing that our resolve and persistence are more significant factors in determining our success than anything else. Other people can help us with parts of what we need to learn or accomplish, but others do not usually have incentives perfectly aligned to accomplish our goals. Furthermore, no one else has enough information to give us a step-by-step guide that accommodates our unique capabilities and situation. We must be our own guide.

There's no greater absurdity than taking everything seriously.
— Baltasar Gracián

We must be able to laugh at ourselves. If we take ourselves too seriously, we will not be as happy as we could be, and it will be difficult for us to admit faults and learn from our mistakes. As we take on big goals and take them very seriously in a sense, we must also be able to laugh at certain aspects of even the most important work and projects in which we engage.

If you would be loved, love and be lovable.
— Benjamin Franklin

When it comes to our relationships with others, we should not expect to get more than we give. If we wish for others to treat us well, we must treat them well. If we wish to have a great partner, we must be a great partner. If we wish to have quality friends, we must be a quality friend.

Keep your eyes wide open before marriage and half shut afterwards.
— *Benjamin Franklin*

If we determine that a relationship we have is worth it overall, we should work to focus more on the positives it brings rather than its negatives. Looking for things to love and praise about the people in our lives helps us deal with the negatives they inevitably bring, too. Letting negatives overly color our feelings toward our friends and loved ones can harm our relationships and our happiness. This way of thinking does not just apply to relationships. It applies to anything that we are already involved with that is still worth sticking with.

Don't criticize them; they are just what we would be under similar circumstances.
— Abraham Lincoln

It is so easy to be wrong about other people. When someone makes a mistake we would not—assuming it truly is a mistake for them—we must consider that the reason may be that they do not fully understand something. Perhaps at some level they understand, but at least some part of them does not fully get it. We too readily believe someone who makes a poor decision is stupid or a bad person, and don't consider the environment and constraints that prevented them from seeing the right decision or prevented them from following through with it. Frequently, we do not give others the benefit of the doubt or put their behavior in the right context.

The former Empress of Russia, Catherine the Great, once said: "The more a man knows, the more he forgives." This is surely true. But it's also true that the more a man simply stops briefly to think before judging—or before accepting his initial judgment—the more he forgives. We must work to form a habit of trying to understand why people do what they do before blaming or judging them.

Nothing can make our life, or the lives of other people,
more beautiful than perpetual kindness.
— Leo Tolstoy

Maintaining a good manner and being friendly and kind to others makes life more pleasant for ourselves and for those we interact with. Having a good manner allows us to feel less distress during otherwise difficult interactions with others. It reduces the likelihood that we will do something out of anger that we later regret. Furthermore, those we treat well are more likely to treat us well, whereas those we are harsh or rude to will generally respond in kind toward us. Additionally, those we treat well will generally be more open to our influence. Moreover, keeping a good manner and having less-confrontational interactions with others makes it easier to back away from wrong positions we acquire by not overly activating our pride.

Criticism, like rain, should be gentle enough to nourish a man's growth without destroying his roots.
— Frank A. Clark

Some criticism of others is necessary, but too much is counterproductive. Being too critical can make people feel beaten down and incapable of improving. It can make people defensive. Being a little more patient, a little kinder when we are critical of others, can make it easier for them to change in needed ways.

There is much we should consider when criticizing others:

- When we must criticize others, we should aim to do so in a way that does not make them believe they cannot overcome the issue due to some immutable flaw that they have. Furthermore, we should not make them feel that they are a bad person because of a fault that they have.

- Instead of directly telling someone how to do something better, we might sometimes consider asking them questions that can lead them to self-discovery, which can be much more powerful.

- When we have to discuss someone's failings, we should work to do so at a time they will be less sensitive and more open to influence—for example, not right after a mistake is made, and not with others around. This will help them focus on how to improve rather than on the poor delivery or timing of our criticism.

- It often makes sense to forgo criticism altogether. Instead, it can be better to praise someone when they make steps in the right direction, even small ones. Over time, this praise can help them take further steps in the right direction. By praising someone for doing the right thing, we may avoid the need to reprimand them for doing the wrong thing.

- We must not come to believe that friends and loved ones are exceptions when it comes to our criticizing them. We must seek to criticize them carefully, perhaps even more so than other people in our lives.

True happiness is to enjoy the present without anxious dependence on the future.
— Seneca

If we live too much for the present, we can end up with a terrible future. However, if we live too much for the future, we can end up with an unfulfilling present, and, consequently, an unfulfilling life. It is very easy for us to establish a pattern in which we focus on future goals to the near-exclusion of enjoyment of the present. We must be careful about waiting to enjoy life until some goal has been accomplished, some pain has completely passed, or some upcoming trial has been overcome. There will always be new goals, pains, and trials. To live well, we must learn to enjoy the present without requiring that everything in our lives first be perfectly in order. We must love the journey and not focus excessively on the destination.

An uneducated person accuses others when he is doing badly; a partly educated person accuses himself; an educated person accuses neither someone else nor himself.
— Epictetus

What does self-compassion entail? Certainly having self-compassion means working to not put too much pressure on ourselves and to not hold ourselves to impossible standards. But it also means going out of our way to be kind to ourselves. We should use kind language and a kind tone with ourselves. We should be kind to ourselves when we discover we don't know something we think we should know. We should be kind to ourselves when we make errors. We should be kind to ourselves as we struggle to improve ourselves, learn new things, and work toward accomplishing big goals.

Living well requires that we be able to see our faults so that we can improve upon them. Self-compassion can help us accept what we have done in the past and who we are now, removing defensiveness that might make us inclined not to see our faults. But we cannot stop there. In accepting ourselves, we must not accept stagnation. We must not accept a life without self-improvement.

Remember not only to say the right thing in the right place, but far more difficult still, to leave unsaid the wrong thing at the tempting moment.
— Benjamin Franklin

We must be cautious about what we say. The temporary satisfaction we get from saying the wrong but tempting thing is outweighed by the consequences. We should value discretion more than most of us do. We should beware of bragging, directly or indirectly. We should beware of divulging secrets—other people's and our own. We must also be very careful about opening up too much about our hopes, fears, or pains to the wrong person.

At times it can be tempting for us to tell lies or half-truths or to deceive others in some way. It is not that this could never be appropriate, but many of us are far too quick to apply lies or deception. We must consider the potential consequences of lies and deception. If we are found out, we can lose a significant amount of trust, which is hard to recover. It is also notable that, in many cases, others need to know the truth more than they need their feelings protected. That said, when we need to say potentially hurtful things, we should try to do so in a way that minimizes the pain while still getting the important points across.

Wisdom has its root in goodness, not goodness its root in wisdom.
— Ralph Waldo Emerson

We should be inspired by the thought of making other people's lives better. However, if we try to help others, without having learned enough about the world, we run the risk of putting our efforts into ineffective or counterproductive methods, even if our intent is good. Often, the best way to improve the world is the more indirect approach of improving ourselves.

Correction does much, but encouragement does more.
— Johann Wolfgang von Goethe

The best effect of any teacher, mentor, book, or program is rarely what they teach us directly. The best effect may be inspiration—helping us believe we can accomplish great things. It might be showing us the importance of learning. Or it might be helping us learn to think for ourselves, allowing us to uncover and challenge more assumptions and discover what is truly important. These effects can lead us to productive self-activity that can carry us far beyond anywhere we could go with only what we are taught directly.

It is easy when we are in prosperity to give advice to the afflicted.
— Aeschylus

As well as we know our own situations, it's hard for us to know what to do in all aspects of our lives. Knowing what others should do in their own lives is even more difficult because we know so much less about their affairs. Sometimes we are tempted to give advice to someone that might work well for us if we were them but might not work for them because they lack important knowledge or qualities that we have. When it comes to big decisions in someone's life, we should give guidance to help them avoid obvious mistakes. However, we generally should be more skeptical than most of us are about our ability to know how others should live their lives. In many cases, instead of giving others direct advice, we might consider providing them with important information they may not know. Combined with everything else they know about their lives, they may be able to make a better decision than either we could make for them or they could make without our contribution.

Be careful whom you associate with. It is human to imitate the habits of those with whom we interact. We inadvertently adopt their interests, their opinions, their values, and their habit of interpreting events.
— Epictetus

We should be very careful whom we spend time with. This is not simply because spending time with the wrong people can involve us in bad situations or make others think less of us. It is also because the wrong people can cause us to lose focus on what is really important and cause us to lose faith in our ability to accomplish great things. It is important to be able to deal with the wrong people where we must, but where possible we should work to avoid them. While working to avoid such people, we should be careful not to consider them irredeemable. Under the right conditions, we should recognize that they are capable of doing better, but it is not our responsibility to help them do so if it comes at a considerable detriment to ourselves.

In contrast, surrounding ourselves with the right people can help us focus on what is truly important. They can help inspire us to do our best and can give us constructive feedback that helps us improve. When it comes to the greatest, most accomplished men and women, it may be difficult for us to surround ourselves physically with them. However, we can get much closer to them by reading their books or their biographies, or by watching videos of talks or seminars they have given.

Keep your face always towards the sunshine—and the shadows will fall behind you.
— *Walt Whitman*

As we work to be realists and to accept the bad in the world, we should also work to have a positive attitude and to be in a good mood. This will not make us fantastically happy and it will not allow us to avoid all negative emotions. But it will make us happier overall by helping us focus more on the good and less on the bad in our lives. Adopting and maintaining a good mood becomes easier with practice, but we should expect it to always take effort.

You should aim to be independent of any one vote, of any one fashion, of any one century.
— Baltasar Gracián

No one person, place, culture, or ideology has all the answers, but we should try to recognize when someone or something has many answers and is great overall. When something has repeatedly brought us closer to the truth, it may be appropriate to pay closer attention to additional answers or applications it may have. However, we have to be cautious about lowering the burden of proof too far, particularly when it comes to important things. For example, we must not get to the point where we accept nearly anything that someone we admire believes without sufficiently reflecting on it ourselves.

It's important for us to have things we are enthusiastic and passionate about, but we can easily become very biased toward such things, seeing primarily their potential benefits and mostly ignoring their potential drawbacks. This bias can also make us dramatically overweight the importance of what we are enthusiastic about relative to other things. For example, a dietician may overweight the role of diet in health while underweighting the role of exercise, relaxation, and interpreting events in less distressing ways. The British statesman Lord Chesterfield once wrote, "When you have found out the prevailing passion of any man, remember never to trust him where that passion is concerned." We must recognize fully that we are subject to this same kind of bias when it comes to things we are passionate about or consider to be a favorite of ours. As best we can, we must work to account for this bias and counteract it.

Compromise makes a good umbrella, but a poor roof; it is temporary expedient, often wise in party politics, almost sure to be unwise in statesmanship.
— James Russell Lowell

In small matters, compromise, even when ineffective for achieving a given goal, may be worth it overall because what is being compromised may not be as important as other things like keeping the people on all sides of an issue reasonably happy. However, in large matters, appeasing all sides may do much more harm than good.

It's important to be able to compromise—to give up some of what we want in order to give others more of what they want. But we must be extraordinarily careful about compromising significantly on the most important aspects of our lives—what we personally need to do to live well. We will regret doing so.

Moderation in all things, especially moderation.
— Unknown, but attributed to multiple authors including
Ralph Waldo Emerson, Oscar Wilde, and Mark Twain

Although we should be careful about exceeding moderation in any area, we should be aware that sometimes moderation is not best. For example, rising to the top of a field requires us to exceed moderation in our practice and study of it. The problem is not exceeding moderation. The problem is allowing the benefits of exceeding moderation in one area of our life to be outweighed by the harm caused to other parts of our life.

It's one thing to set daily goals to follow most of the time, but it's another to insist on hitting the target every day. For example, it may be healthy to typically sleep 7-8 hours a night, but some days it is not reasonable to expect this much sleep. Trying to follow such rules of thumb inflexibly can make us needlessly anxious as it is simply not practical. Furthermore, even if we could reasonably follow such rules of thumb every day, it may not be as healthy as allowing more variance. For example, it may be healthier to occasionally fast, than to try to eat the same calculated number of calories every day.

Experience is only half of experience.
— Johann Wolfgang von Goethe

To understand the world better, we can't just be present for a lot of experiences. To learn, we need experience, but that's not all we need. Reflection is another crucial ingredient. Everyone learns from experience, but some learn much more than others. To make the most of our experiences we have to think deeply about them, trying to understand why things happened the way they did and searching for specific ways to improve our actions in similar future situations.

You cannot do wrong without suffering wrong.
— Ralph Waldo Emerson

If we harm others, we must expect to be harmed by them or those sympathetic to them, punished by the worry about this potential harm, or punished by regret. What seems to be in our self-interest often is not. Sometimes such things can help us in some superficial way and harm us in more important ways. For example, gaining wealth by harming others is not worth it. As the philosopher, Epicurus noted, "It is better for you to be free of fear and lying on a bed of straw than to own a couch of gold and lavish table and yet have no peace of mind."

We must be careful about justifying anything we want to do by pointing to the moral rule of our choice. We must remember that something that is moral in one way may be immoral in another way. For example, in some cases, helping someone significantly may prevent them from critical self-development. There is a lot of value in thinking carefully about the best actions to take, but we cannot be overly reliant on rules, even moral or ethical ones, as we do so.

True wisdom comes to each of us when we realize how little we understand about life, ourselves, and the world around us.
— Socrates

There is much we should consider regarding our ignorance of the world:

- As complex as the world is, the answer to so many questions we encounter should be "I don't know" or "I'm not sure" or "I need to get more information." For many problems, even after much research and careful consideration, it is still appropriate to be unsure of a solution. Too frequently, our discomfort with uncertainty leads to error. Requiring certainty can cause us to make logical leaps that we should not. It makes us more likely to oversimplify situations, downplaying or missing important factors we need to account for to make wise decisions. Requiring certainty makes us more likely to apply a general rule without enough consideration given to the possibility that the situation before us is an exception to this rule. When we encounter difficult problems, we should look for possible solutions, but we should not insist on immediate, complete answers. By doing more investigating and staying more open-minded, we are less likely to commit ourselves to wrong beliefs that, once acquired, are difficult to escape from, and we are more likely to get to a more complete answer eventually.

- We often have strong opinions on subjects we really don't know that much about. We should re-evaluate many of our opinions. We must work to determine when we don't know enough about a topic to have an educated opinion about it. When we notice this, we must sometimes seek more information about the subject so that we can acquire a more enlightened opinion on it. However, when it comes to some topics, we must realize that even after considerable research, we may still not know enough to confidently take one side or another.

- It is helpful to conceive of humility the right way. Humility is not doubting ourselves but believing in our abilities the *right* amount, having a good grasp of what we do and do not know, what we can and cannot do. Humility is not being confident about things we should not be confident about. It helps to be confident about our potential, but we should not be confident we are already great at something if we are not yet great at it. And we should not be overly confident that we can *quickly* come up with sufficient solutions to difficult problems, even though we can solve many such problems after enough time and effort.

- Even after we are much more aware of our ignorance than most people, we must still fight the tendency to think we understand much more than we do. Reminding ourselves of how little we know is a lifelong duty, and it is a crucial one.

True knowledge lies in knowing how to live.
— Baltasar Gracián

It takes a considerable amount of knowledge to be wise, but one can be very knowledgeable without being wise. Wisdom requires a certain kind of knowledge that should be differentiated from other types of knowledge. Knowledge tells us about the world. Knowledge helps us accomplish goals. So does wisdom, but wisdom also helps us choose and prioritize our goals. Being wise means knowing how to live overall, not just when it comes to certain aspects of life.

Conviction is worthless unless it is converted into conduct.
— Thomas Carlyle

For us to benefit from beliefs and ideas, we cannot just recognize their importance. Beliefs and ideas that don't lead us to act or prepare us for potentially needed action are not of value. We should aim to learn how to live well, but more importantly, we should aim to actually live well. When we encounter a good idea, we should be careful not to simply say "I know that," even if at some level we do know it. Instead, we should make sure that we are actually applying the idea as well as we should. The philosopher Voltaire once observed that "Common sense is not so common." It is worth clarifying that intellectually understanding commonsense things is common, but following through on them often is not.

In life, the trick is not so much to know what to do—it is getting ourselves to do what we know. We can only do this by engaging the part of us that knows what to do. To do so, it helps to take the time to think and reflect. It helps to ask ourselves powerful questions such as "What am I trying to accomplish?" or "What is the long-term impact?" or "What are some other options?" or "What could make this go wrong?" It is also helpful to look at actions we have already taken and ask questions like "What could I have done differently?" or "How could this have been better?" The hope is that such questions will engage the part of us that knows how to answer them well.

It is human nature to think wisely and act in an absurd fashion.
— Anatole France

A wise person can know that they are wise, but they must appreciate that wisdom is a relative thing. Even if we are much wiser than most, we are still far from perfectly wise or perfectly able to make good decisions. As the French writer Nicolas Chamfort once noted, "[E]ven in a wise man there is more folly than wisdom." Many of us would be wiser than most people if we did not think ourselves to be much wiser than we actually are and accounted for this in our decisions. The wise are aware that they have very foolish parts to them and do their best to mitigate the damage these foolish parts can cause.

We must never believe that we exist entirely independent of our environments or our basic instinctual drives. We must admit to the potentially negative influence of our environments and instincts. Under poor enough conditions, we are all capable of bad behavior. We should not be too confident about our ability to exercise wisdom in poor conditions like being surrounded by temptation, being tired or hungry, or being in a very emotional state. Believing otherwise puts us at more risk by causing us not to take precautions we should such as avoiding situations in which we would be influenced negatively. If we know when we can't be wise, we can mitigate the risk of doing something foolish. For example, to try to eat healthier, we might not buy sweets rather than have them readily available and depend on our willpower to prevent us from overconsuming them. As another example, we might not discuss a sensitive issue with a friend or family member when we are tired or upset, as opposed to doing so anyway and working hard to control our emotions.

Health is so necessary to all the duties, as well as pleasures of life, that the crime of squandering it is equal to the folly.
— Samuel Johnson

There is much for us to consider regarding health:

- To a large degree, a healthy body is necessary for a healthy mind. And to a large degree, a healthy mind is necessary for a healthy body. We must not neglect either, or we are neglecting both. The ability to live well and make wise decisions is largely contingent on both good mental and physical health. As we work to become or remain healthy, we must remember not to take the pursuit of health to the extreme or be too inflexible with applying our healthy habits, as this is unhealthy.

- We live in a time in which it can be easier to treat the symptoms of many health problems than to tackle their underlying causes. We must not succumb to treating only symptoms when treating the underlying cause is reasonably possible, as we will find much greater relief and better health in the long run by doing so.

- Health is not fully in our control. To the extent we are disabled by bad health that we cannot remedy, we must work to accept it. In such cases, we must focus on what we can do, not on what we cannot do. If when it comes to our health, we are dealt a bad hand, we must work to live as well as we can given our constraints.

The discovery of truth is prevented more effectively, not by the false appearance things present and which mislead into error, not directly by weakness of the reasoning powers, but by preconceived opinion, by prejudice.
— Arthur Schopenhauer

The world is very complex, and it's easy for us to end up believing things that are wrong or incomplete. Unfortunately, our problem is not just that we adopt false or incomplete beliefs, it is that we often become nearly positive that they are correct and complete without enough reason to be so sure. Once we become sure of something, we can set unbelievably high bars for the amount of evidence it takes for us change our mind. If we aren't already sure of something, we can much more effectively take in future information and appropriately adapt our beliefs.

Sometimes our beliefs are totally wrong. More often, our beliefs have some truth to them but are incomplete or need certain modifications. Recognizing that our beliefs often do not have to be totally scrapped, but instead need tweaking, can help us be more open to examining them closely, which helps us to improve upon them.

We may despair of knowing, we must not despair of judging.
— *Anatole France*

Wisdom is knowing what *can* happen, good or bad, and reacting appropriately to it. It is not predicting precisely what will happen in any given situation, but being able to respond appropriately to the *possibilities*. This means taking reasonable actions according to the events that *could* happen. To take reasonable actions, we need to have some idea of the possibilities and the *rough* likelihood of each, but we cannot allow the most likely outcome to completely drive our decision-making. Our beliefs about what is likely true should be differentiated from our beliefs about what we should *do* with this information. An action with a small chance of a very bad outcome may mean we avoid the risk, even if it means giving up the likely outcome of a small gain. Conversely, an action that has a small chance of resulting in an amazingly good outcome but a high chance of small loss may be worth proceeding with.

Rather than try to make no mistakes, we should try to make no big mistakes. As we consider our beliefs and what actions to take, we should ask the question, "what if we are wrong?" If the outcome is disastrous if we are wrong, we may need to consider setting the bar really high for how certain we have to be to proceed without at least taking some additional precautions.

In life, we can prepare for potential negative events, but we should make sure that that the precautions we take are worth it. If greatly reducing the chance of a negative event significantly increases the odds of a different negative event, it may not be worth it. For example, we might greatly decrease our risk of dying in a wreck by never driving, but we might tremendously increase our risk of having a lower-quality life due to the severe limitations we would have. In this way, taking less risk in one area of our lives can increase risk in other areas. Sometimes this tradeoff is worth it, but sometimes it is not.

No man was ever wise by chance.
— Seneca

The Greek philosopher Heraclitus once wrote: "Applicants for wisdom do what I have done: inquire within." As Heraclitus knew, no one reaches the highest levels of wisdom simply by stumbling on one wise source that teaches them everything they need to know. No one reaches the highest levels of wisdom purely by having the good fortune to have quality experiences. The highest levels of wisdom only come to those who take ownership of their own development of wisdom, who seek to acquire it from many sources and reflect considerably on both what they learn and what they experience. One only reaches the pinnacle of wisdom by climbing a little every day. A powerful method for making this ascent is to continuously ask and answer the question, "How do I live my life a little bit better?"

The pursuit, even of the best things, ought to be calm and tranquil.
— *Marcus Cicero*

The wise pursue great things at the same time that they pursue a quiet mind. The loss of peace of mind and inner calmness is not often worth the gain we might get from engaging in a frantic, stressful pace or putting great pressure on ourselves. We should have the flexibility to occasionally give up our calmness and tranquility in pursuit of something great, but we should set a high bar for doing so. And we should not be doing so but rarely. Generally, even the actions we take to make our lives calmer and more tranquil in the future should themselves be calm and tranquil! If our life is not tranquil enough, we will waste energy that we need to conserve to act wisely when it really counts. If our life is not tranquil enough, we will be unhappy even if we know how to live well in many other important ways.

It is not always by plugging away at a difficulty and sticking to it that one overcomes it; often it is by working on the one next to it. Some things and some people have to be approached obliquely, at an angle.
— André Gide

Many of life's most bothersome problems do not have to upset us as much as they do. Many do not need to be solved the way we want them to be. Consider a problem we may create for ourselves: how to get as many of the finer things in life as possible. This might be very difficult to achieve. We would do better not to solve this problem directly but to take the more effective but indirect approach of learning to be more grateful for what we already have. Consider another example. Perhaps our problem is how to live a very long life and to make ourselves feel nearly guaranteed to do so. This is no easy task. What is easier and will certainly make us happier is to accept that the length of our life is not guaranteed and to learn to focus more on the quality of our life than on its length.

Nine-tenths of wisdom is being wise in time.
— Theodore Roosevelt

Wisdom is not about avoiding all mistakes. One can be very wise and make many small mistakes. The wise minimize big mistakes. One of the best ways to do so is to stop little mistakes from becoming big mistakes. We have to think ahead, allowing ourselves to get off bad paths as quickly as possible. We must quit making the same mistakes repeatedly. We must apologize when we hurt others. We must give ourselves the flexibility to change our minds when necessary, even about important topics. And we must be able to move on from calamities and keep living life well.

Thank You

I want to thank you for reading my book. As I wrote in the introduction, I hope that my book helps put you on a path to living better and better. I wish for you to have many wonderful experiences, enjoying life now and not living solely for the future.

Going forward, I hope that you think a lot. I hope that this thinking helps you to more clearly see where your knowledge ends and your ignorance begins. May you direct your thoughts not toward solving problems but toward solving the right problems. May you direct your thoughts not toward building a case for what you or other people want to believe but toward finding truth. And very importantly, as you work to make the best of the truth you find, remember to smile and laugh often and to not take anything more seriously than you should.

A Request

I would greatly appreciate you taking a moment to review this book on Amazon.

Thank you again for reading my book!

Made in the
USA
Columbia, SC